The Moon, The Tide, and All I Tried

EL HOFFMAN

To myself, because I know that I deserve better, and to my readers, because I know that you do, too.

A NOTE TO READERS

As with all of my writing, this collection comes from a place of honesty. *The Moon, The Tide, and All I Tried* explores love, grief, and survival in greater depth than my previous works. At times, it depicts the raw pain of loss and heartbreak. It is also the most loving, beautiful, and special thing I've ever written.

This collection also introduces several characters who may return in future poetic or prose works. Together, they form part of the broader universe that connects my writing.

I put a lot of emotion into *The Moon, The Tide, and All I Tried*, and I hope you'll love it as much as I do.

PRAISE

"With raw honesty and lyrical grace, *The Moon, The Tide, and All I Tried* is a stirring poetry collection that tenderly navigates the emotional ebb and flow of love, loss, and healing, offering readers solace in shared survival." — NewInBooks

CONTENT WARNING

This book contains mild strong language, along with sexual suggestiveness and references to substance use, sexual assault, eating disorders, trauma, grief, mental health, and suicidal thoughts. While these subjects are explored through an artistic lens, reader discretion is advised.

Love and Pain: All the Same

"Under the Same Moon"

One of the only things that provides comfort to me
is knowing that even if we don't speak,
we still see the same moon at night,
the same stars,
and the same sun during the day.
You are there with me,
even if you are not here.

"Kneel"

I feel like a puppy
waiting for its master,
who will blindly follow his lead,
no matter what he says or does,
how long he's gone,
or where he's been.
When he returns to me,
I'm sitting there
with my tongue out,
and my tail wagging.

"Viewing My Story"

Please don't keep viewing my story,
if you don't want to be there for me.

"Love at First Sight"

I had
love at first sight,
but, due to circumstances outside of my control,
we never saw each other again.
I don't know if I
will ever be okay with that.

"Is It Really Different?"

This is so different, you say,
before abandoning me
in the middle of broad day.

"Unfinished Business"

The only thing left unfinished
is our story.

"Tactile Hallucinations"

All the time,
I feel my watch vibrate,
thinking you had reached out.
Each time,
I am wrong.

"To Be Safe"

I looked for you there, to be safe,
but you weren't there.
And, deep down, I feel like a disgrace,
even though I know I am not.

"Like Haifa"

Somewhere that feels like Haifa,
but not somewhere that feels like you.

"Starting Anew"

I think that's why
when I met you,
my life changed irrevocably.

"You But Not You"

If you want to compartmentalize,
then so can I.
The person that I fell in love with
and the person that you are,
are two different people.
You are not the person that I love,
and the person that I love is not you.

"Ruining My Day"

I was actually having a pretty good day,
until I saw you and entered a state of dismay.

"Unresponsive"

They say actions speak louder than words.
In this case, you're doing neither.
I'm broken and bruised,
and you're unresponsive.

"Belonging to No One"

If you belong to the world,
how could you ever belong to anyone?

"Gratitude Attitude"

If your gratitude
comes with an attitude,
then I would rather be on a different latitude
than deal with your platitude.

"I Don't Exist"

I don't know how you can tell someone that you
     love them,
and then pretend they never existed—
it's cruel.

"*Duality*"

I have two memories burned into my mind now:

You, at first sight,
and you, during your betrayal.

Both are equally vivid.
Both are equally weighted.

"My Greatest Treasure"

I pick pennies up off the ground
and other than your love,
they are my greatest treasure.

"Actions Have Consequences"

It wasn't your fault,
but it was a direct result of your actions.

"Potentially Worth It"

You took everything away from me,
but it's fine if we're meant to be—
even if it shouldn't be.

"Lack of Compassion"

If you can't be there for me
after my injury,
then you don't get to be near me
or hear me.

"They Won't Believe Me"

But I won't say anything,
can't reveal what happened—
not that anyone would believe me, regardless.
But I don't understand your mistreatment.

"The Great Salt Lake"

Trapped and stuck in this space,
yet you were my saving grace
at the Great Salt Lake.

"Praise God"

I need to worship God,
not magic—
unless it is the magic I feel
when I am with you.

"Or So I Thought"

When we met the first time,
we experienced love at first sight.
Who would have thought?
Then things fell apart
because you weren't ready.

And then, out of nowhere,
fate intervened, or so I thought.
We saw each other again.
You felt nothing.
But I felt everything.

I tried to keep my cool
and not let anyone see my cards.
At first, I thought it was okay.
But I am not.
And I cannot sleep.

"Under the Same Roof"

Ignore me all you'd like,
but that doesn't change the fact that we're in the
same building.

"Okay"

I will probably never see you again,
and that's okay.

"Monogamy"

If you are dating
the internet,
then I am not interested
in dating you.

"Lies and Ex-Boyfriends"

I don't think you're a liar.
But at the same time,
I do feel lied to.

"Spend My Days Alone"

I would rather spend my days alone
than ever go through
what you put me through
again.

"Dread"

Your voice is still in my head,
even when it fills me with dread.

"I Lost You"

I looked into your eyes,
and their cold indifference made me realize
that I had lost you.

"Not That Far From Me"

Digging my toes into the sand,
wishing that we walked on the same land.
Looking at different waves in the same sea,
knowing that you're not that far from me.

"Not an NPC"

I'm not an NPC in your story,
I'm a real person.

"Stand With Me"

I was hoping you would
step up
for me
and not
ask me to
step down
from you

"My Silent Plea"

I wish you wanted me
like I want you

"Stay and See"

I wanted to learn everything about you,
not how to live without you

"Touching a Frame"

I need to touch you
and feel your warmth—
know if what I felt is real.
But my fingers keep tapping glass,
unable to pass.
I just want the real thing, at last.

"Not What I Expected"

You were...
not what I expected.

" Heartbreak "

Heartbreak is
devastation in the core of your being.

"Gratitude Attitude v2"

If your supposed gratitude
is really an attitude,
then I would rather live on a different latitude
than hear your platitude.

"A Pattern"

Someone pointed out a pattern to me today,
and I deserve better.
You do too.

"Literal Thinking"

You say that I think too literally,
but I don't know how to think figuratively.

"This Trip"

On this trip,
at this event,
in this building,
within these walls,
will occur
either the greatest decision
or the worst decision
I have ever made.
No in-between,
no middle ground.

"Yes, I'm Going"

Yes, I'm here.
Yes, I'm going.
I had the opportunity.
I couldn't not go.
I had to shuffle things around.
I went through multiple forms of torture.
I couldn't not go,
so I'm here and I'm going.

"Through the Glass and Dominoes"

I can't get up,
I'm struggling.
Falling, unable to put pressure—
leaning against the glass.

I get up.
Through the glass, I see you—
an ass.
Smiling, laughing, chatting.
While I'm aching from the chain you started,
and the pain that stuck around.

"Mentally Spoken For"

They all say I could find something better,
but how?

Would the air feel more weighted?
Would their face be more burned into my mind?
I will always remember the exact tilt of his head,
and his exact facial expression.

I remember exactly how the air felt—
how *everything* felt between us.
I will always remember that,
and nothing could ever compare.

That choice I made
gave me *more* clarity, not less.
I don't want another.
Not after that.
Not after him.

"In My Head"

Maybe eventually
I will buy myself a wedding band,
because I'm committed to the memory
of a ghost—
a person who never truly existed.

"Wedding Bells"

No, I have never been married,
and as of right now,
I never intend to.

"Grand Reveal"

Day zero.
The morning of
the end of the countdown
to the big surprise—
the grand reveal.
I hope you'll appreciate.

"*True*"

You can keep saying things,
but it doesn't make them true.

"You're Not Listening"

Stay with me,
love me,
grow with me,
she said to the brick wall.

"Masquerade"

I miss
who I thought you were.

" Light the Way at Night "

The candelabra is supposed to light the way,
yet I find myself bending to everything you say—
and then you move the goalpost
one step farther away.

"You"

But I don't want better,
I want you.

"This Isn't Working"

I don't think this is working.
The fact of the matter is,
I want to be your partner,
but you don't want to be mine.

"Losing You"

When I love someone,
and I feel like I'm starting to lose them,
it's the saddest thing.
Right when I start to feel like I have you,
you fall through my grasp.

"Crossing the Street"

I need to cross the street,
but the sign spells out the letters of your name.
I feel like I'm being mocked—
by the universe,
or by the city.

"Away on a Beach"

It is strange in some ways,
but a piece of me is with you—
in a place I've never been,
on beaches I've never seen,
in a restaurant I've only heard of,
and on forested trails I've never walked
at a state park I've never visited.
I wish you could be in my arms—
here, and not there.
Or me in yours—
there, and not here.

"Does Life Go On?"

I am learning to live without you,
in the blackest of nights, and through the greyest of
    days.
Always, and forever,
until the day I die.

"Here Saved Me"

We told each other that we wanted to meet here,
    together,
many times, that one night.
But you went without me,
and now I'm here without you.
And yet, I still think of you,
what here meant to me, to us,
and what this could have looked like for us,
together.
I don't know when or if I'll see you again, my
    friend,
but I will always think of you when I think of here,
and know that you and it saved me.
So thank you,
but if only it could have saved you and us, too...

"A Gift"

I wasn't sure if you would come here to see me,
but I had brought a gift with me regardless—
or perhaps an offering.

"My Life and Joy"

But I don't sleep anymore—
not without you in my arms
The promise of you
here
with me
is gone
and with it,
went my joy.

"Insomnia and Chocolate"

I haven't slept since the night that you left me,
and chocolate has become the best friend that I
didn't need.

"A City, or Your Arms?"

Waiting for this city to save me,
but wanting to be in your arms all the same.

"Any Questions"

You're probably mad that I didn't ask you any
    questions,
but you never gave me the opportunity to.

"I See You Everywhere"

I saw someone that looks like you,
with the same expression in their eyes,
but it wasn't you,
because you wouldn't be here,
and you wouldn't do what that person was doing.

"I Don't Believe"

I refuse to believe
that all of this happened
only so I could write a few lines.
There must be another explanation for this
    pantomime.

"Under the Surface"

You were cold and callous,
while masquerading as warm and inviting.

"Long Distance"

I do not want to be your phone girlfriend,
I want to breathe your air and touch you.

"Not Forever"

Soulmates are both made and found.
Having love at first sight doesn't always mean
    you'll have love forever.
Life doesn't work that way.

"*Thunderstorms*"

You were the only person I had ever met that liked
    thunderstorms,
and now pangs of thunder and flashes of lightning
    bring your face to mind.

"I See It Now"

I saw a side of you
that I had never expected to see.

"All of Me"

If you don't want all of me,
then you don't get a piece of me.

"We Happened"

You were real
We were real
We happened
And I'm not crazy for wanting to hold on to the
   memory of that

"No Matter What"

I write about love at first sight,
because I've experienced it.
It was the best
and, frankly, worst
thing I've ever experienced.
In spite of this, I wouldn't undo it for anything,
no matter what.

"I Deserve Better"

I will always love you
and remember how I felt,
but I know that I deserve better.

"Undeserved Cruelty"

Don't be cruel to me
for being kind
to you.

"Thanks"

I got all the closure I needed,
thanks.

"Actually Grateful"

Oh, no, don't worry,
I will find someone
who's actually grateful,
or I will be content
to be alone.

"In My Thoughts"

And when I finally feel like I'm over you,
there you are—
in my thoughts.

"Mr. Doodyhead"

I wish that you were the one losing your mind
    instead,
Mr. Doodyhead.

On Life: A Different Kind of Pain

"So Much More"

I went through some things recently
that made me appreciate
what I have
so much more.

"Love Story"

I went to the ice cream shop,
and I fell in love.

"The Outcome"

I cannot control the outcome of a situation,
only the preparation.

"Strength"

I am no longer going to diminish myself
to appease others.

"Modern Technology"

You once told me
that I was your "right hand to computering,"
and now,
I can't look at modern technology
without thinking of you.

"Resilience"

Well,
this
has certainly
taught me a lesson
in resilience.

"Cute vs. Cuter"

Cute dog,
cuter human.

"Into Your Orbit"

I don't want to fall
back
into your orbit.

"Live in a City"

I think that I want to live in a city
with hills
and chocolate cupcakes.

"Miscommunication"

You're mad about my communication,
you tell everyone except me.

"God Called Me to be a Writer"

I'm okay with hitting pause
God called me to be a writer
And I don't want to put it off
It's my life's purpose
And my joy
I love my career
And I feel like God called me to that too
But right now, God is calling me to write
So I'm going to hit pause
I don't know what will happen long-term
But I'm grateful regardless

"Acceptance is Everything"

I have learned to accept
that I might always be alone.

"Mentally Not Single"

Legally I am single,
emotionally I am not.

"Belonging to No One"

A lot of times, with men,
they appear so gentle and kind and wonderful,
when out and about or in a group setting,
and then behind closed doors...

"Unraveling Fast"

The loop is closed,
the threads are knotted,
yet my sanity is unraveling fast.

"This Chapter Has Ended"

I closed two chapters today,
and for that I am grateful.

"Don't Misrepresent Yourself"

If you want someone to know and love the
    real you,
don't misrepresent yourself.
Be who you really are, always.

"Plausibly Deniable"

Willfully obtuse,
willfully obtuse,
willfully obtuse.

"Who is Amber?"

Who is Amber?
You asked me if I was there to see her
But I don't know who that is
You didn't tell me who she is,
or why you thought I was there for her
I don't know who Amber is
Who is Amber?

"Charm"

I can't ask to come back a third time,
because charm doesn't work that way.

"A Change of Plans"

I had to abruptly change my plans,
but that's okay.

"Former Driver"

It's all ads, static, or Spanish
You'll realize I intentionally forgot how to operate
every part of a car

"Undiagnosed Autism"

Stop fidgeting.
You're so smart,
but you talk too much.
It runs in the family,
they said.
Stop doing that,
please act this way instead.
That was how I learned to mask.

"One Day At a Time"

Follow your heart,
and be proud of yourself for trying.

"Convincing"

I can convince myself of anything,
except that I am fine.

"Cookies"

You mock me
because I'm not cookie cutter,
but we're different types of cookies.
Chocolate chip and frosted sugar
both eat the same.

"Is It Actually Sunny?"

It is sunny out today,
so I should be happy.
But inside, it is cloudy,
so I am not.

"Sibling Spat"

Have you ever heard of
a sister-induced
migraine?

"Splitting"

Equally certain
about two unequal things.
My mind is equally certain,
as if someone tied my hands
with string to each side.
Bouncing back and forth
between the two things—
I cannot make a decision,
so back and forth I go.

"I Am Moving"

I am moving,
but I do not know where.
Downsizing I am doing,
so I feel prepared.
But where am I going,
perhaps other than to Somewheresville, IDK?
Definitely within the USA.

"Safe Spaces"

We are all unique individuals
I value being in spaces
where everyone is accepted
as they are

"Figurative Felines"

Well, the cat's out of the bag,
but at least it's not in a cradle.

"Floating Through Space"

I feel like a shapeless, amorphous blob,
floating through space—
with no purpose,
and for no reason,
but I know I am not a disgrace.

"Spilled Secrets"

I learned a lesson today:
Don't trust someone who has been drinking with
    your secrets
unless you want them spilled.

"Mrs. Divinity Learner"

Mrs. I'm better than you
Mrs. Don't trust a doctor, trust me
Mrs. I'm pretending, but to my every whim you
    must be bending
Mrs. Filling my cup by pouring out yours
Mrs. Logically inconsistent, but why are you so
    resistant?
Mrs. Making up biblical fan fiction,
yet no one else is really Christian
Mrs. Divinity Learner

"Walking Ghost"

If I look haunted,
like a walking ghost,
it's because I am.

"Sober-minded"

She has always related to how the Bible says to be
    "sober-minded,"
choosing not to engage with mind-altering
    substances
such as alcohol.

"A Rush for Time"

Also,
would you be okay with me getting brunch?

"A Writer's Life"

Even if I am not writing,
I am selling my writing,
marketing my writing,
or thinking about my writing.
I am always involved with my writing.

"A Coffee Chain"

Don't say that you hate chains
if you call your favorite the same nickname I do.
You go there daily,
far more often than me.

"Don't Choke Me"

Consent is key,
so please don't choke me.

"Toxic Cycle"

Unblock,
reblock,
unblock,
reblock.

"All I Have"

For better or for worse,
you are all I have.

"Mindreader"

I struggle to read social cues,
but you expect me to read minds?

"Moment of Realization"

That moment of realization
when you realize you can write about it.
Your hopes and dreams?
Jot them down.
What you wish could happen?
Fictionalize it.

"On the Beach"

Not me,
surprised to feel and see
the sand beneath my feet
on the beach.

"Judgment"

If you're going to put quotation marks around my
    suffering,
you won't hear of it.

"The Void"

If anyone needs me,
I will be screaming into the void.

"You Don't Know Them"

I don't want to explain,
because I don't think you know the person,
and it's a long story

"Blanket Statements"

I do not make blanket statements—
most advice applies to me and me only.

"Mug"

I am missing one mug
I cannot find it
Which mug do you think it is?
I hope it is somewhere
Never mind...
I found it.

"Waterfall"

She passes by the great waterfall
Rising much higher to compensate,
throwing herself to one side
She turns trying to avoid the water,
able to pass by.

"Out of My Element"

What is a car?
Is it like a horse-drawn carriage,
but autonomous?
Or is it fueled like a steam engine?
Does it just take you where you need to go,
Does it know to take you where you need to go,
or do you need to think about it?

"Understand the Chances"

I can sometimes
give second chances,
but under no circumstances
do I give third chances.

"Confusion"

The confusion was intentional.
Intentional confusion of oneself,
interesting choice.

"Sad Birthday"

I won't wish you a happy birthday,
because I would prefer to wish you a sad birthday.
But I don't lie,
and I mask to fit in.

"Right Place, Right Time"

Do you ever just feel
that you're in the right place
at the right time?

"New Information"

I still don't know
what to do with this information.

"The Right to Opinions"

Everyone has a right to their opinion,
even if it's logically inconsistent.

"They Don't Talk to You"

You act the way that you do,
and then wonder why they don't talk to you.

"Mental Health"

Struggling to get out of bed,
too many thoughts running through my head.

"Don't Take it for Granted"

It's interesting that
now I take looking at bananas for granted again.

"Allergies"

Allergies!
Then I sneeze.
Cough and hack,
and then I wheeze.

"Hit On"

I don't hit on anyone,
they hit on me.

"I See the Appeal"

I now see the appeal
of turtlenecks
with fitted sleeves.

"To the Point of"

I'm taking the meaning behind this song
far too literally.

"*Loud is Not Correct*"

Being loud
is not the same
as being correct

"Accomodations"

We shouldn't be afraid
to ask for accommodations.

"Cliche"

Looking at myself,
twirling my hair in the mirror.
Things are not as they appear—
how could this be cliche?
When this is who I am—
this is my life.

"Winners and Losers"

I did it because I let him win,
but I won't do that again.

"Mr. Wedding Ring"

You're so amazing,
you tell me,
while spinning your wedding ring.

You don't tell me that you're married,
you don't mention your wife,
you don't mention anything at all,
except how amazing I am.

You throw compliments at me,
like a soccer player throws balls.

It isn't until I ask,
that I learn your marriage
is a multi-task,
Mr. Wedding Ring.

"Poetry is a Message"

Poetry is often a message that someone needs in that moment.

"Delusional"

You know you're delusional when...

"To Break a Promise"

I broke a promise today—
one I made in a state of dismay,
many years past.
But there is no "at last,"
as I don't want to see you again—
I don't want your ask
to come to pass.

"Worldly Woman"

Oh, worldly woman, defile me,
they said, while getting down on one knee.
But no, I don't want to defile you,
all I want is love that is true.

So go back from whence you came,
you are asked to be chaste.
Don't let me be the reason you don't do as you are
    asked.

The great state with a cutout in the northeast
    corner
offers you far more than me, your warner.

"Swamp Demon"

You walked into the room,
uninvited,
unwelcome,
unwanted,
disheveled,
dripping water,
kelp stuck in your hair,
your dress torn to shreds,
gaping black holes for eyes,
and wearing a witch hat,
yet no one remembers but me.

"*Time Continuum*"

Things are not as they seem,
yet they are very important.
Maybe time is just stretching,
but low-key.

"*Wow*"

Well,
oh well.

"New Job"

Where and how do I
track my time?

"The Opposite of Love"

Time bleeds faster than I can swim.
I hoped everything would be bright,
but now I can't see through the dark.
How are things winding right, if they are winding
     away from me?
My eyes have lost their light,
and as for when, the answer is likely never.

"I Want Out"

Another night,
another manipulation.

"Family Dynamics"

But here's the thing—
you don't get to kick me out of the family
because you don't like me,
if everyone else does.

"*Tourism*"

I am a traveler,
not a tourist.

"*Flattery*"

I like your flattery,
but that doesn't mean I want
it
or
you.

"Not Your Gathering"

I remember the harassment,
I remember hearing you were no longer welcome,
and you came anyway,
out of disrespect,
rather than reverence.

"That Question"

In more ways than one,
and especially would not under the sun,
I regret asking that question.

"There"

I learned that I can't live there—
it is beautiful,
but not for me.

"Creature"

I always said
that if I came home
and found a creature inside,
I would leave and it is their home now—
until I came home to you.

"Grieving the Living"

I never thought that I would need
to grieve someone
who is
still alive.

"Terrible Person"

I'm glad that I didn't waste the rest of my life
on a terrible person.

"A Queen Forever"

Looking down through a sewer grate,
then walking over the panel,
I fall in.
The world below is better than I expected—
or deserved.
I am a queen,
but a queen *forever*,
if you know what I mean.

"The Moon Above

And in the end,
I am alone.
But the moon is above me,
crescent and bold,
stories untold,
forever cold.

The moon is above me,
and I sure tried—
I survived
the spring tide.

Acknowledgments

I would like to thank Sam Bolano for his work as my illustrator. I would also like to thank my readers for allowing my vision to take root in your minds, as this collection means a great deal to me.

While *The Moon, The Tide, and All I Tried* introduced more pain to my writing than I had previously expressed, I also injected a lot more humor. Had I not experienced what I did, this would have been a different collection of poetry. For that, I am grateful, as those experiences gave me the inspiration to write this.

Other than "Allergies," which I wrote as a child and previously published in my elementary school's newspaper, as well as in *The Ever-Dark*, and "The Opposite of Love" which I only finalized this year, everything was written throughout 2025.

I hope you enjoyed *The Moon, The Tide, and All I Tried*. If you did, please consider leaving a review on Amazon and/or Goodreads, and if you'd like to read further, my first collection, *The Mirror, The Mask, and All I Ask*, is also available.

As a child, I once sang "goodbye" in my sleep, about the loss of an imagined red balloon. In that spirit, goodbye for now.

About the Author

El Hoffman (born February 8, 2000) is an author, poet, and data expert. A lifelong writer, she debuted with *The Ever-Dark*, a literary fantasy novella. She is also the author of the contemporary romance novelette *No Other Reason* and two poetry collections: *The Mirror, The Mask, and All I Ask* and *The Moon, The Tide, and All I Tried*.

Outside of fiction, El has built a successful career implementing HubSpot for businesses and earned her Master of Science in Data Analytics from Eastern University in 2024.

When she's not writing or working, she enjoys reading ebooks, taking long walks, and hula hooping. She's also passionate about video games, cooking, exploring new restaurants, and traveling.

instagram.com/elhoffmanauthor

tiktok.com/@elhoffmanauthor

amazon.com/author/elhoffman

linkedin.com/in/elhoffmanauthor

bookbub.com/authors/el-hoffman

threads.com/@elhoffmanauthor

youtube.com/@elhoffmanauthor